ADAM
and the
DANGER *of* SLEEP

ADAM
and the
DANGER *of* SLEEP

POEMS

Thomas Ronald Vaughan

RESOURCE *Publications* • Eugene, Oregon

ADAM AND THE DANGER OF SLEEP
Poems

Copyright © 2022 Thomas Ronald Vaughan. All rights reserved. Except for brief quotations in critical publications or reviews, no part of this book may be reproduced in any manner without prior written permission from the publisher. Write: Permissions, Wipf and Stock Publishers, 199 W. 8th Ave., Suite 3, Eugene, OR 97401.

Resource Publications
An Imprint of Wipf and Stock Publishers
199 W. 8th Ave., Suite 3
Eugene, OR 97401

www.wipfandstock.com

PAPERBACK ISBN: 978-1-6667-3867-4
HARDCOVER ISBN: 978-1-6667-9968-2
EBOOK ISBN: 978-1-6667-9969-9

MARCH 7, 2022 12:51 PM

Contents

FOR LENNIE (after John Steinbeck)	1
PROPHECY OF SAINT PETER	2
BLUE BIRD	3
ENTER BY THE STRAIGHT WAY	4
PUSH, AND THEY WILL FALL	5
THE POET ON DEATH ROW	6
MAFIA CONSPIRACY	7
RESCUE DOG	8
PSYCHOTIC BREAK	9
PETER AND CATHERINE MARSHALL	10
WANDERING JEW	11
IDENTICAL SNOWFLAKES	12
UNAMUNO	13
TWO FLIES	14
BLACK DAHLIA	15
ALTERED PERSPECTIVE	16
DAILY GRACE	17

THE SHEPHERDS' FAREWELL TO THE HOLY FAMILY	18
THE WORKS OF EDWARD HOPPER	19
FAMILY HOME	20
THE INNOCENT ENABLERS	21
WISE SOLOMON	22
THE SENSE OF HOLDING EACH OTHER	23
EVENING REGRET	24
A FUNERAL TO REMEMBER	25
CHANGED LIFE	26
CALLING ON THE "PREACHER"	27
ART IMITATING LIFE	28
SPANISH INFLUENZA	29
THE VIRGIN IN A BOTTLE	30
A LONELY HEART	31
TO AN EAGLE	32
WORSHIP	33
UNSEEN PILOT	34
THE MEN WHO KNEW	35
CAIN BENDS OVER ABEL	36
EVERY RIVER HAS A PAST	37
THE LEDGE	38
THE COMING OF JACOB MARLEY	39
RECRUITING THE VICTIMS	40

SURVIVING CLERICAL ABUSE	41
PHILOSOPHY (for Wittgenstein)	42
CRIMINALS IN LOVE	43
PSALM FOR MY FOOTBALL TEAM	44
SNOW WALK	45
THE HUNTER	46
ADVENT	49
TAPERS	50
FIGHTING *COTINIS NITIDA*	51
FAILED RESCUE	52
THE O'CONNOR PEACOCKS	53
THE MEANING OF FLOWERS	54
CHILD SOLDIERS	55
TO LUCASTA, WHO NEVER WAS	56
ELIZABETHAN IMITATION: TO A FLAME ON A LOG	57
LIFE AMONG WALRUSES	58
THE BLUE CHILDREN	59
ENDING IT	60
MARIS GOES DEEP TO RIGHT	62
TO HOPKINS	63
AMERICA GOES TO WAR, 1917	64
DEPRESSION	65
EMPTY SPACES	66

TRANSITORY ONES	67
FOR THE LUFTWAFFE DEAD	68
FINAL TALK	69
COMING STORM	70
THE COMPACT	71
IN PRISON, PAUL THINKS OF STEPHEN	72
FOR W. D. SNODGRASS	73
ANTIETAM, 1862	74
THE CHURCH	75
A FASHION SHOW OF GHOSTS	76
THE STERN FATHER	77
THE MOST MEMORABLE DAY	78
PORPOISES ESCORT BODY TO SHORE	79
FRANKENSTEIN	80
NAAMAN IS CURED	81
THE WINDOW	82
THE ROOM	83
IN THE DARK WOOD	84
THE TABLEAU	85
FALLING INTO MONA LISA	86
EVOLUTION: THE DAWN OF TIME	87
ADAM AND THE DANGER OF SLEEP	89

FOR LENNIE (after John Steinbeck)

It is a truth universally acknowledged
That a man should be allowed
To shoot his own dog,
Especially one who cannot possess
The tenderest things
Without crushing them to death.
Even if there is no absolute intention,
You must say, "Look over there,
And I will tell you the story again."
Then, the gun is discharged,
And the simple, wretched thing
Falls lifeless to the waiting earth.
It is all a form of innocence,
For he is family,
And no one is guilty,
Or, perhaps, everyone is,
And will always be.

> John Steinbeck, (1902–1968), American author,
> wrote OF MICE AND MEN.

PROPHECY OF SAINT PETER

They say I will soon be upside down
Because I claim certain things to be the case.
They will do what they will do,
And after all, I am a very old man.
I contain horizons.
I would say this before I depart,
And, see, they are coming now:
Beware and be forewarned, my dears,
For, from my experience I must conclude
That we always lose faith, sputter,
And begin to sink
In the most familiar waters.
For God's sake, do not look at the storm!

According to tradition, the Apostle Peter was crucified upside down. In Gospel stories, he attempted, unsuccessfully, to walk on water going to Jesus Christ.

BLUE BIRD

Down the overhung river,
Skimming just above water,
Came the small blue heron,
Gliding,
Deliberate,
Intentional,
Delicate.

ENTER BY THE STRAIGHT WAY

My mind runs in a circle,
And sees itself come back,
Like trains in an amusement park
Enrailed on rounded track.

But when it meets itself again,
It hardly can discern
The slightest trace of anything
Experienced or learned.

And so I go through life's alarms
Consumed by sad remorse
That none so slovenly can find
The straight and narrow course.

Matthew 7:13: "Go in through the narrow gate", quoting Jesus.

PUSH, AND THEY WILL FALL

If you can get your enemies
To stand erect,
So that their ankles touch;
If you can get them to join
In long, lean lines;
If you can get them
To hold in their arms
Massive, heavy rocks—
If you can do that,
You can push,
And they will fall.

THE POET ON DEATH ROW

They think that I am here for love,
But I am here for hate.
I now write words to flutter hearts
And not those to berate.

I own I did the foul deed;
Twelve men agreed with me.
But mercy was not to be found;
No words could set me free.

Tonight I leave my books of verse;
The Chaplain will be kind.
Tomorrow opening my cell
Dark stories will he find.

MAFIA CONSPIRACY

Sitting alone at the long bar,
He could not be spoken to
By the loud men, the flirting girls,
Or the suggestive, erotic themes
On the prints in the gaudy, golden frames.
He could not be spoken to
Except by the Spirit in the spirits
Which told him he had done the right thing,
And should well do it again.
He could not be spoken to
Even as he now brushed shoulders
With the one true friend
Who had quickly retrieved the shovel and pick,
Thinking he might hear an explanation tonight
Or more likely never.
They could not be spoken to
As they sat at the shiny wood bar,
Mesmerized by the rich amber
Flowing into each small glass,
An excellent single barrel Tennessee whisky.
They could not be spoken to,
Nor would they speak.

RESCUE DOG

Ordinarily, you do not respond
To cacophonous yelpers
Who bite and lick promiscuously
Without regard for who has money
And who does not.
Omnipotently, you stand among cages,
Nothing much in mind
Except the gnawing, snipping fact
That in your life and house
You have space,
Can create sanctuary,
Need someone to talk to.
As you muse, the atonal symphony wraps all in stereo.
Then, completely unlike yourself,
You open generous arms
And shout, "Come unto me!"
Now thoughtfully defining criteria,
In the Election of Grace,
You calmly choose.
A ransom is paid, accounts settled,
And all is waggingly well.
You are off.
In the eternal scheme of things
One is saved.

PSYCHOTIC BREAK

The child was lost for two hours
But turned up at school just fine.
Yet, you went completely insane
And have not been here since.
What did you lose and when
To cause such complete deterioration
In those short minutes?
We can find no one who knows
Or has a clue.
Tell me, sad lady:
Who will mother your precious son
While you are away?

PETER AND CATHERINE MARSHALL

When Peter Marshall told Catherine,
"I will see you later, my Dear,"
He actually would not.
His heart would not let him.
So, the great Scottish Presbyterian
Slipped gently into eternity
With an impressive homiletical genius
To share with saintly listeners above.
He left his brilliant wife not quite alone,
For she caressed an unending pen
With which to produce
Her inexhaustible corpus
Of deathless faith.

Peter Marshall, (1902–1949); Catherine Marshall, (1914–1983).
She wrote A MAN CALLED PETER.

WANDERING JEW

One day in old Vienna
Stephan Zweig and friend
Walked past a stall
Selling Medieval chests.
Zweig asked seriously,
"Which ones had belonged to Jews?"
The bewildered man responded
He did not know.
The exile, the sad, the tearful Austrian,
Between laughing and crying,
The *fernweh-heimweh,* replied,
"The ones with wheels."

        Zweig (1881–1942) and his wife, Lotte, exiled from Nazi
            Europe, committed suicide in South America.

IDENTICAL SNOWFLAKES

Yes, I am very sure
That last year at this time
Under the microscope
I saw the same design.

And so it falls to me
To right the ancient lie,
For nature can indeed
Its own self multiply.

> "It is unlikely that any two snowflakes are alike due to the 10 quintillion water molecules which may make them up."
> Atmospheric Science "fact".

UNAMUNO

Unamuno said that Christianity is *agonia*,
One simple example being Spanish Catholic crosses
Which display the Corpus
In the throes of writhing pain.
We Protestants prefer
The shiny, empty ones,
But must be careful not to imply
That it wasn't so bad anyway,
Or that He really was crucified
Between two gently flickering candles.

Miguel de Unamuno, (1864–1936), Spanish author and philosopher, wrote THE AGONY OF CHRISTIANITY.

TWO FLIES

She flicked the fly out of the soup,
It landed in the tea.
"Be damned," she shouted in anger.
"Be damned," the fly agreed.

"Why speak you thus?" she asked him.
"And why you so?" said he.
"The soup was for my husband;
The tea I bought for me."

BLACK DAHLIA

Of all animals in the Kingdom,
I am told that vultures have the best sense of smell.
From miles away
They can locate the carrion,
Then form a "wake" or a "kettle"
Or even a "committee."
The wake, it seems, is the group feeding,
And today's attraction is a
Twenty-three year old actress,
As lovely as any filmed alive,
Which, dismembered, she is not.
Death by horrendous murder
Is indiscriminate at best,
And though I might comment on
The unmitigated horror, or
The beauty in the eyes of the birds
With foreboding wings,
I will simply note that
They are coming.
Neither they nor the authorities
Know why she is here.

      Though occurring in 1947, the murder remains unsolved.

ALTERED PERSPECTIVE

O,
Once
You see
Snakes
In a tree,
You look at
Limbs
Quite
Differently.

DAILY GRACE

Intent upon contentment,
I steal my life away,
In books to lands and legends,
But find I cannot stay.

For each time at the closing
Of tale or myth or lore,
My life again comes calling
With a demanding chore.

But as I shoulder skyward
The burden of the day,
I sense contentment gather
To sweep despair away.

THE SHEPHERDS' FAREWELL
TO THE HOLY FAMILY

We leave you at this time of brutal cold,
Though it is not our choice to rise and go.
It is the animals we now must save.
Our bones tell us there will be wind and snow.

We have no way to say what we have seen;
We are unlearned men, without the words.
Our only conversation often is
To shout a friendly greeting from these herds.

We have a sacred calling from the Lord.
It is our duty, so we must away.
But after all of mystery and awe--
The wonder of each ordinary day!

THE WORKS OF EDWARD HOPPER

In his paintings, the stories will not end well
For no one is talking,
Or making contact with any eye.
Someone sits on the side of a suggestive bed
While the partner pretends to sleep,
Or in another a man sips warm coffee
While the sexual friend can only stare and frown.
Hopper the Tall, six foot five,
From up there sees
That despite the multitude of screaming millions,
We are dangerously alone
And must daily take our emotional pulse
Or fall, spinning,
Into the semi-dark abyss
Of an other-worldly, forbidding café.

                        Edward Hopper, (1882–1967), American artist,
                                  painted THE NIGHTHAWKS.

FAMILY HOME

Clocks chime in these old-smelling rooms
As I sit in Grandmother's empty house.
It was a better world then, I affirm.
She is dead and I am not,
But when it comes for me
I will leave neither a room nor a clock
Nor an aroma of being
In one place seventy-six years.
What is wrong with me?
Did I have to go so far
And wander rootless in the world?
I simply did.
Now, as I rise, look around,
Breathe deep and go,
I am only a man
Taking a moment's interlude,
Thinking thoughts, wiping tears.
One more time, one more glance.
"Good-bye", I mumble to myself,
And close the ancient door.
The house is sold.

THE INNOCENT ENABLERS

When they pumped her stomach,
She roused and said
It should be remembered
Only as a foolish accident.
They did nothing to prevent
The next attempt which went
Well beyond sleeping pills,
Open oven doors,
And to this plunge into
Dark, deep water, thick with ice.
The cause of death had something
To do with not being able to breathe
In such unhealthy, frigid temperatures,
Which everybody had wondered about anyway,
If such a misstep should actually occur.

WISE SOLOMON

Live, and soon the pulsing years
Shall bend before the cosmic spheres.
Twisted fingers, twisting toes.
Slow, how slow the old one goes.

Solomon, before he died,
Pushed the earthly things aside,
Claimed that what he lost in beauty
Reappeared in holy duty.

> 2 Chronicles 9:23: "Kings consulted him to hear the wisdom God had given him."

THE SENSE OF HOLDING EACH OTHER

In Cartesian epistemology,
One can absent incarnation
And do almost anything.
That is mostly a grand formula
For hopeless insanity.
But I must admit
That when I flew
On several rockets,
And viewed the earth below,
I was much the saner for it,
And knew that if we do not
Reach out and hold hands
We will all fall off.

EVENING REGRET

The night was filled with bursting stars,
I saw her to the door.
I think of it, and always will:
I should have kissed her more.

A FUNERAL TO REMEMBER

There must be a poem in all of this:
The way they carted you off,
The way you stayed those awful weeks
And grieved yourself to death.
The mysterious past,
The breakdown of the family,
The insulation against suffering---
All relevant topics here.

You were unlovely.
The drawing arthritis
Turns toes and fingers outward.
True enough.
And they were embarrassed, in truth.
So, no holidays, no cards; all common courtesies ceased.

You clung so well.
No murmuring, no pity—until the end.
Then it all fell apart
And you could not kill forsakenness.

When those children came to "claim" you,
They talked and laughed too loud.
You rested in the casket
With a strange and enigmatic smile.

CHANGED LIFE

A gathering of flowers,
A friend we lay to rest.
The coffin lowers slowly;
So ends his painful quest.

This man had wanted fortune,
He lived to garner fame.
But on his way to grasp them
Another claimant came.

He was quite overpowered,
Then turned his life around.
And so it is a servant
I place into the ground.

The flowers will be wilting,
Soon dry and blow away.
But I know well who lies here;
I signal, "Let us pray."

CALLING ON THE "PREACHER"

A woman came to the parsonage yesterday,
And among other things she said
She'd never seen an African American
Who couldn't dance or play ball.
I chided her with unministerial rage.
Nonplussed, she whimpered away
Even as we both knew
There are no black people in her "Church,"
And no black *people* in her world.

ART IMITATING LIFE

In this poem,
The main characters,
The important people,
The gifted and talented,
The truly good,
Are killed off first.
And some would want it
Just like that.

SPANISH INFLUENZA

I think it is a big mistake
To tell people to dig
In the graves on Svalbard,
Because, well, they just might free the virus
And start another pandemic.
I have the fantasy of each night's news
Ending with a word about some bug
Out there somewhere
Because somebody turned over
The wrong rock,
Or cut the wrong tree.

When I was a teenager
I counted seven graves in a row,
All with the same month, a date, and 1918.
I found out later
That even machine guns
Did not kill men that fast.
But then, gratefully, one morning,
Like the war,
It was over.
I found out something else:
One of REVELATION's hot Riders *should* have been "Plague."
Now, I often put my head to the ground
And just listen.

THE VIRGIN IN A BOTTLE

In 1870's Germany, the Virgin Mary
Appeared inside several bottles,
And naturally caused quite a stir.
One was ink, one medicine.
Apparently, she helped you write
Or made you well.
It seems very clear
That not even *Kulturkampf*
Could keep her away
From pious souls
Who understood well
That dioceses and governments,
To the contrary notwithstanding,
Faith lives best
In hearth and home.
So cleave the wood
Or open the cabinet
And miraculously she was there!
In my experience, the Virgin Mary
Can be downright devilish
When it comes
To keeping the rules
About when to show up, or where.

Kulturkampf was a late 19th century culture war between the government of Prussia and the Roman Catholic Church.

A LONELY HEART

It cannot be wondered why Mr. Singer
Committed suicide in his bleak room
At the boarding house.
One should remember
That he was a deaf mute, a Jew,
In a Southern mill town, 1930's,
Rejected by the girl next door;
That his black physician friend
Was dying of cancer;
And the obese, mentally ill man
He visited at the insane asylum
Died and was buried
Without as much as a word to him whatsoever.
I allow him such grief, frustration,
And visceral pain,
That I doubt he even
Heard the shot as he fell
Across the small iron bed,
And died in his dismal space
Which was growing smaller every day.

Characters from THE HEART IS A LONELY HUNTER,
a novel by Southern writer Carson McCullers (1917–1967).

TO AN EAGLE

I cannot fathom this hunting bird.
Gripping the craggy rock at food time,
He spreads wings like a loose fan
And braves the cold wind's strong rebuff.
High and soaring, with eye down,
He spies the prey,
And descends in precise and deliberate fall
Like no man-made thing.
To stay the shattering crash, he brakes,
And with a fell thrust
Talons the shrieking foe.
Then, in one majestic move,
He rises from the killing scene,
The day's provision secure
Among that dripping armament.

WORSHIP

"Hallelujah!" and at that sign
We hail Her Lord of space and time.

"Praise Him!" and at that thought
We name the wonders he has wrought.

"Our Father," and at that prayer
We cast on Him our every care.

"Amen! Amen!" and at that word
We turn again to the Absurd.

UNSEEN PILOT

You tried not to discover
An island on which to land.
But there was a Pilot
You did not see.
He took your hand in Springtime
And led you straight to me.

THE MEN WHO KNEW

I am told that in World War II
Thousands of G. I.s, to their tearful
Wives, sweethearts, and mothers,
Said, "I won't be coming back,"
To which the girls replied,
"Of course you will,
And I'll be waiting for you."
But they did not return
And in order to see them
Women had to go to France
Or some nameless Pacific island.
Very few chose to make that trip,
And I don't blame them, after all,
For a man who's going to die,
Tells you so,
Kisses you tenderly,
Then gets on the train,
Has left a more indelible impression
On the heart
Than the exercise of walking through
Rows of crosses
Until you stop,
Take a deep breath, and
Trembling, say,
"Here he is."

CAIN BENDS OVER ABEL

He tugged and tussled
With the bloody boy
Until he realized
He must go home
And tell his parents
That new words were needed
For their crude and brutish vocabulary,
And that he could also
Do this to animals
He would rather not contend with,
Being stubborn.

        Genesis 4:8: " . . . Cain turned on his brother, and killed him."

EVERY RIVER HAS A PAST

Do not believe that centuries upstream
The river looks like this.
I can take you to a place
Where we can hold hands, run,
And jump it together.
Come with me, then,
And I will show you Hope.

THE LEDGE

As a paraplegic
She was stolen from her life
And family
In a fall that would
Make a humorous video.
But what concrete did not know was this:
It could crush a T 5,
And one intolerable day lead her
To the ledge of a tall, familiar building,
From which she would roll,
Knowing full well
She could not fly.

THE COMING OF JACOB MARLEY

How clanged those chains in that material mind.
Settling in his unbelief, Scrooge mocked and scoffed the visitation
Which, as physical, could have been beef or cheese.
But it would not desist.
The roar of that miserable spirit
Cut its introspective road.
Scrooge cowered and shook in his subjectivity.
The night would be a night of death and rebirth,
For those rough chains cracked and split
The locks and keys on one man's dark soul
And opened that impenetrable fortress
To the ravages of joy.

Characters from A CHRISTMAS CAROL, by Charles Dickens,
(1812–1870), English novelist.

RECRUITING THE VICTIMS

When young men dream of nothing,
And that is what they do,
They have no way of knowing
Their dreams cannot come true.

They hear of war and fighting.
They say they will not go.
But shamed, they stop their dreaming,
And join the youth laid low.

SURVIVING CLERICAL ABUSE

Before him in the casket
Lay the touching sweep of years,
And the one of eternal confusion.
Now, in the child's mind,
Much older,
The intrapsychic merges:
Love and hate, reason and unreason, life and death.
The sad, brave victim
Actually hopes to see him again
In a happier, less violent time.
Then, in the plush-toy room,
He had absolutely no idea
What was unctuously and insidiously coming.

PHILOSOPHY (for Wittgenstein)

Philosophy is like fishing:
Going into the water,
Coming out.
Casting into the trees,
Getting caught.
Knotting the line,
Fretting, untangling.
Throwing again and again.
Philosophy is hitting the spot,
Feeling the strike,
The yank, the reel.
It is the pleasure, the pain, the doubt.
Philosophy is the doing.
It is not the fish . . . . . .

Ludwig Wittgenstein (1889–1951),
influential Austrian philosopher.

CRIMINALS IN LOVE

They argued about many things;
So many times she cried.
He was an open, "honest" man,
But many times he lied.

He lied because he loved her true
And if he told her all,
She would be hunted as was he,
And not survive the "fall."

And so, upon a moonstruck heath
The final truth was said.
It sent two lovers far away,
To join the truthful dead.

PSALM FOR MY FOOTBALL TEAM

O God,
They are worse than I ever imagined!
They cannot punt,
They cannot pass,
They cannot kick, except each other.
They *can* run—thank you for that.
But mostly they run after other players,
Trying to catch the swift backs
Who break into the clear, time after time.
Give them wings on their youthful feet!
Give them alertness.
They are dull.
Give them memory to remember the snap count.
Help our quarterback to only fade,
Not completely away.
Renew his strength after each sack.
Bless the coach who pants like a hart,
And rails at the officials—it is not their fault.
And bless me in my misery,
As I sit game after game
Learning again with David,
At least once a week,
That my enemies will rise up against me
And they shall surely prevail.
Selah.

SNOW WALK

I left one sunny morning.
I had no where to go.
The temperature was falling;
I took no thought of snow.

But as I blithely wandered,
The sky began to gray.
Yet I enjoyed the turning
Of Winter's darkening day.

When flakes began to flutter
I turned to realize
That I had lost my bearing
Under now frightful skies.

Since then I wander daily
To find where I have been,
But think it does not matter:
The snow and I begin.

THE HUNTER

> . . . the hunter's sense of understanding with the hunted animal . . .
> interests me also.
> —JAMES DICKEY

I lean against the trunk of this thick tree
And watch the uneasy prancing,
The troubled jerks of your magnificent head
Which I can sever as a proud trophy.
You are out-matched, out-witted
By my machinery and methods.
You know you are stalked,
You, who have not stalked,
But fed along the river greenage.
Your armor deceives.
You are no slayer of beasts,
Or ripper of flesh,
No jungle terror.
But I have come to slay you.
In my coat is the intrinsic right
To fix my sights on your neck
And break your tough hide,
To crumple you with one shot
And stand in exaltation like young David.
You owe me nothing but our encounter.
For this, I have traveled days.
I have killed more of your kind than I remember.
      Now you turn toward my position,
And with weak eyes strain to assess
This upright creature who threatens.
I step from my cover not to mock or defy,

But to reveal who it is
That has come for this ceremony.
You acknowledge my gesture by stomping,
By thrusting the heavy horn toward the wind.
I raise my gun.
It will not be still.
My hands are wet.
Sweat beads on my brow.
"Cover yourself, you fool!",
I hear myself shout.
You respond only by rotating,
Angling toward me, as if to invite
A better, more deadly shot.
You step, slowly, toward the mysterious blur
Who speaks nonsense or shouts for help.
But you have not known me.
      I squeeze, and it is perfect.
You are shocked to your knees
And already dead before the stiff posts
Give way under your crushing hulk.
The dust puffs to your thud.
Dead limbs crack as you collapse and roll.
Sounds die and the stale air clears.
I must begin.
I walk to your place,
Fall to the ground,
And embrace the bleeding neck.
I extend to prostrate beside you in the sand
And press my body to yours.
Closer, closer, we fit.
I tremble, I laugh,
I weep.
My God, how I have loved you!

My wet eyes close.
We are one.
Above, the diamond African sky
Seems to stretch away forever.

                        James Dickey, (1923–1997), Southern American poet,
                                          and author of DELIVERANCE.

ADVENT

The Magi in their finery
A desert highway trod,
Convinced they were ambassadors,
The plaintiffs for their God.

The star, the star so brightly shone,
It gave a soothing light.
But when it made its Westward way
It left the darkest night.

But Christmas does not come so clear,
It only comes in gray.
And babies in the manger stall
Look up and look away.

TAPERS

I seek no startling illumination.
These are for dark places
Of mystery, awe, and faith,
Which have succored all accretions
Of doubt and pain and joy.
I simply light them here,
Asking.

FIGHTING *COTINIS NITIDA*

I had always thought of June Bugs
In terms of color—
Delicate, jewel-like backs,
The most compelling green.
Until this Summer when I learned
That some months ago
They had used my yard for an incubator,
Emerged, and mastered the skies
In such profusion that they
Actually collide in mid-air.
Unable to sun or walk without attack,
I am re-thinking June Bugs.
I have wished for yard birds
Or cats to dispatch them
With a quick smack.
When dead, they are as beautiful
As I remember in my youthful farm days.
A wiser man now,
I sweep them up
Drop them in the trash,
Quite proud of my ability
To view even this innocent invasion
In terms of its own natural mystery.

FAILED RESCUE

There is no one in the boat
But young lifeguard rowers.
The child, the wave—it was too much.
Frightening to think where they go,
Those lost to this roiling chaos.
Planes go down, ships go down,
And nine-year old children with only one arm
Go down as well.
Sometimes, when the surf is fierce,
And you cannot swim,
You may join that vast, diverse civilization
About which those standing on the shore
Now wonder if it is truly desirous
To hope that one day
This sea will give them up.

Revelation 20:13: "Then the sea gave up its dead."

THE O'CONNOR PEACOCKS

If, in the middle of the night,
You have ever heard
The shrilling cry of a peacock,
You could wonder how she could write
Anything of real merit.
Then add the slow debilitation from Lupus,
Which had also killed her father.
As a good Roman Catholic
She took it all with Stoic resolve,
Aided by frequent Mass.
And for years the Church has flirted
With putting her in the queue for sainthood.
This will never happen
Because her subjects were too raw,
Her language too Southern,
Much, much too saucy.
Afterward, her mother took care of the peacocks.

Flannery O'Connor, (1925–1964), Southern American novelist

THE MEANING OF FLOWERS

The flowers in my garden
Awaken with the dawn.
They have a voice proclaiming
They cannot be here long.

But in their blissful moment
They brighten all the earth,
And teach the nodding living
To bloom before their death.

I languish in the sunshine,
Then note the flowers play.
Enlivened by their vibrance
I turn and dance away.

CHILD SOLDIERS

A bomb falls outside the village.
The small boy does not move, he does not hear.
"Soldiers!" someone cries. He strains to listen.
His head turns in the direction of the noise,
But his eyes never leave the ground.
Shots are fired nearby. He no longer cares.
The bloated stomach, protruding elbows,
Skin stretched over bones tighter than a drum
Will not let him.
The fight ensues.
The soft, brown eyes are still wide.
They stare at the ground which is very near.
The sand was stirred by his last breath
And formed a small ridge in front of his mouth.
There are two holes in his back,
Two punctures which give color.
He looks asleep, but even in sleep he cannot close his eyes.
Lullaby. Good night. Rest now, my little one.
The child soldiers walk away.
They talk—Kalashnikovs, booty, the next attack.
Hot barrels are smoking in the sun.
This village is quiet. This war is won.

Agencies estimate there are as many as 200,000
child soldiers in 20 conflict zones.

TO LUCASTA, WHO NEVER WAS

He could not love so dear, so much,
Loved not he honor more.
But for some silly English feuds
He went away to war.

And once returned, he wrote to her
The verse that made his name.
But she was a composite lass
To his poetic shame.

'Tis true Lucasta never lived,
And never scanned a line,
But she has lived for centuries
In Richard's loveless mind.

English poet, Richard Lovelace (1617–1657),
wrote TO LUCASTA, GOING TO THE WARRES.

ELIZABETHAN IMITATION: TO A FLAME ON A LOG

Dance high, O Thou hot demon of the coals,
And turn from blue to yellow in Thy flight.
Dance higher still until Thy might is told;
Come from Thy home and warm me in my night.
Steal on, O wretched thief of endless time!
Mock Thy prey and smile with fiery lashes.
Turn life to death to life; commit Thy crime.
Change her hundred years of pride to ashes.
What would she be if Thou weren't co complete;
A rest for robin, even home for man?
So small, but lethal measure dost thou mete.
Engulf, destroy her with Thy wicked band!

Though now so soft and pure, I'll not touch Thee,
But do I pray with unseen hand, touch me.

LIFE AMONG WALRUSES

He rippled on the shore
Back in his fattest hour.
Breezes bore him on and up.
He accomplished:
Pushed five sons to life,
Ate fish off the deepest shoals.
Moonlight saw him baring tusks,
Finest ivory, stiffest beard.
His strong tail flapped miles
Across the grainy sand.
The last of his days
He bellowed to mother,
Chased three young into the sea,
Stopped, turned in his tracks, and butted.
Three foul clubs crushed his adamant skull.
There was a storm
In rage against the rocks.

THE BLUE CHILDREN

In my dream the beautiful girl
Slogs across the burning desert
While screaming birds dip and dive.
Undeterred she moves toward the blue children
Who hold in their hands water,
Which, gleefully thrown into air,
Turns the desert into a paradise of green.
The birds can only sit and caw and mock.
The beautiful girl sees all and then moves past.
The children hold hands and watch motionless,
As so beautifully, she becomes a woman,
Only one shimmering point,
Then disappears.

ENDING IT

So it has come to this,
Some coffee in a booth
Where we have met before
And I will sorely miss.

Your eyes are just as blue,
Your hands as beautiful.
I will not touch them now,
I know what hands can do.

But may I think of these,
Your hands, your eyes, your heart,
When we are through with this
And back with those we please?

Against these numbing scenes,
A man more logical
Would loudly shout his piece,
And say what all this means.

I would want you to know,
If I can summarize,
Our all too brief affair:
It went where it would go.

And as we turn away
To do our senseless things,
I know that I have found
One place my heart could stay.

So take this with you, then,
And think of it as I
Descend to the dark land
Where hearts can never mend.

MARIS GOES DEEP TO RIGHT

Just before he hit 61
My cousin got his autograph
On the wrapper from a piece of Wrigley's gum.
We had taken the ferry from Norfolk to Baltimore,
Said we'd rather see the Yankees,
Took a Greyhound Bus to D. C.
And the Shoreham Hotel.
The Yankees were there, too.
We ran into Skowron, Bauer, and Maris.
Our fathers were alcoholics,
But we could talk baseball all day.
I always wanted Maris to stay with the Indians,
But I was way to shy to ask.
I think I had no paper.
We went to the better game,
And next day took the ferry home.
In the middle of the night,
I rolled over
And watched the somber Chesapeake Bay lighthouses
Go solemnly by.

New York Yankee baseball players. Maris was the first to break the single season homerun record of Babe Ruth.

TO HOPKINS

I am undisciplined, base, vain.
My lines are undisciplined and mostly do not rhyme.
But you come to me when I am at my worst,
My champion, my sterling priest,
My Jesuit, my worldly monk,
My earthy mystic steeped in God.
I crush my paper with a blast of words
Which you, Father, taught me.
But in that we are far, far removed.
When my lines die their pressy death,
Your lines will be pressing out poets still.
You must be troubled to discover
That God did not care
If you published your pungent verse.

Gerard Manley Hopkins, (1844–1889), English poet,
whose verse was collected and published only in 1918.
He had burned many of his manuscripts.

AMERICA GOES TO WAR, 1917

The ships of war bear their sons away
Amid weeping and waving of flags.
It is a glorious thing to fight for one's dreams!
But on the field of battle the dreams give way
To the horror and carnage of hate.
It is surely vanity of vanities.
All ideals, families, hopes disappear
From minds that strive to kill or die.
As trenches fill, young men grow old.
This most morally ambiguous war
Is never won, though the ground
Shifts like a jigsaw puzzle.
The youths are lost.
Pictures and films of their vacant eyes
Bring home the hovering guilt.
One should not ask a soldier things like that:
They vote to outlaw war who never fought.

DEPRESSION

A person who is depressed enough
Can have what looks like thought disorder.
We should know that
Because we have all been
In that trough
Where the whole world seemed
Incongruous, shattered,
Completely out of joint,
And we acted like it was.

EMPTY SPACES

Sweep the house clean and demons come
Unless the rooms are full
Of spiritual realities
Ethereal and dull.

Cf. Matthew 12:44, Luke 11:24:
Parable of the Return of an Evil Spirit

TRANSITORY ONES

What happens in the Springtime
Must not be noised abroad.
The sap rises to treetops
And young men practice words.

They practice them in speeches
For girls along the way.
They seem profound, original.
It is the month of May.

But never say I told you,
The words have all been said.
And he who wooed so coyly
And she he wooed are dead.

FOR THE LUFTWAFFE DEAD

I would not go into that sky today,
For Goering is insane,
And the Spitfires will trail you
With ruthless staccato.
You are no match for them.
For you, this is an incidental, another trophy.
But those pilots count different days.
Backed against the North Atlantic,
Europe in chains,
They will meet your might with
A sense of destiny.
They will dive at your Dornier,
Straight into your tight formation,
Pilots with only six or eight hours in the air.
       I can see you roaring to war
In strict, horizontal sets.
The Spitfires come.
You fight.
They come again and again.
It is too much.
An engine fails, a gunner slumps.
You break formation downward,
Begin to smoke,
And mark a perpendicular on the sea.

        During the Battle of Britain, the German Air Force,
          under Hermann Goering, lost over 1700 planes.

FINAL TALK

Do not press me for answers
That I am loathe to give.
We had the conversation;
So best to live, let live.

We *had* the conversation.
I *do* recall it well.
No more from me is needed.
I have no more to tell.

No! I recall, *correctly*;
I listen when I'm told
That everything is different
And all the past is old.

In labyrinthine regions
Beyond this Land of Word,
Emotions hang like flowers:
We spoke and both were heard.

COMING STORM

I would like to go toward that dark cloud
Split now by hot, yellow streaks.
The green of trees stand out, bold,
Bristling up for this coming storm.
They will be bathed in cold, hard rain.

Thunder grumbles like gas in a belly
Too full not to move.
Sharp crackles sigh, relieved after a long roar.

I would like to go to that dark cloud
And swing upward to the mouth of water,
To the point where vapors seize the dust,
Distill, and fall to earth, far below.

Alchemists struggled years for such a key,
So inaccessible to them, and me.

THE COMPACT

He pulled the trigger slowly.
The clock struck 3 AM.
The place of love and lovers
Was lost to her and him.

IN PRISON, PAUL THINKS OF STEPHEN

Acts 8:1 "... And Saul was consenting to his death."

I remember standing behind Mother,
At her left shoulder,
Looking out over the shallow, brackish lake.
We did not speak.
I remember waves moving with the hot wind,
Dancing in ripples, wave and circle,
Circle and wave.
I remember turning to leave,
That awful correspondence in my pouch,
Veins pounding in my head,
Blood dripping from my hands,
Clothing strewn at my dusty feet.
I did notice with particular delight
The arch of stones the old men threw.
Unable to be arrows, more like lobs,
From weakened, stringy arms.
They rose and fell.
Fell and rose.
But in my dreams I do not go.
My mother calls.
I do not ride.
There is no Christ.
I am not there.

> Saul, converted to Christianity, became Paul,
> and always grieved persecuting believers.

FOR W. D. SNODGRASS

Thank you for splitting your heart with a whack
And tying up the pieces for sale
At a marketplace that asked for none.
They were so amazed,
You won the Prize!
I tell you, no prize winner,
The reflection in reverse
Cuts deep, too.
I never leave her
But she goes away,
Growing up.
You understand.

        American poet, W.D. Snodgrass, (1926–2009),
        wrote Pulitzer winning, HEART'S NEEDLE,
        about divorce and his daughter.

ANTIETAM, 1862

"Just keep your wits about you, men.
It's only musket shot.
They cannot kill the whole of us,"
He said, and then he dropped.

And so died Sergeant Willingham;
A better man than he
Had never led his lads to war,
Nor died so needlessly.

The most casualties of any one-day battle of the War Between the States, 23,000 killed or wounded, with unclear outcome.

THE CHURCH

Plying the waves, what a fantastic conglomeration!
We do not see eye to eye.
We cannot say our hearts.
We lounge and tease at calm wind.
We huddle together when storms come.
Through the journeys of all time,
This ship fathers and mothers the millions.
Though Hell's jaws spit fire,
It will float!
It will prevail!

    Cf. Matthew 16: 18: "The Gates of Hell shall not prevail . . ."

A FASHION SHOW OF GHOSTS

They dress for the occasion and they strut.
They dip and spin showing me things
I had not seen before.
Making contact with their veiny eyes,
I notice something strange, significant :
They now fear me!
It is because I sit and watch,
Am quite unmoved,
Have nothing more to do with them.
They are not as ghoulish as I supposed,
And I should have been kinder to some.
But those were ancient times,
And I was sad,
And did not know
That nothing much was out there
After all.
These ghosts were only mine, internally.

THE STERN FATHER

The father lies intestate in a room
Of heavy curtains, adding to the gloom.
The children were not ever welcome here.
There was not much expansion in this tomb.

He gurgles with no noticeable rhyme,
Not even as the clock begins to chime.
Coincidence, without a single tear,
As every head is turned, noting the time.

It does not really matter in this case,
For he was not an asset to his race,
Nor to the oldest son who now comes near
To pull the wrinkled sheet over his face.

THE MOST MEMORABLE DAY

On any other day it would have been impossible.
But not today.
Today, the children were jumping rope
Near the large tree,
And the old man was watching with tears in his eyes.
It would have been impossible,
But the storm came up and thunder clapped,
And everyone scampered away to a safe place
In the dark stairway.
The old man fell, and called for help
Which never came.
And it would not have happened any other day,
But with thunder, lightning, and rain,
And all the children away,
The old man knew that today
It was not only possible,
But would happen,
And he would never again see
Children jumping rope,
Or a dark cloud,
Or a safe place which would be
Quite enough.

PORPOISES ESCORT BODY TO SHORE

Four hours after he drowned
Three porpoises left their pod
And nudged the body back to shallow water.
It was then retrieved by searchers.
The large and reliable Sheriff Austin saw it happen.
"Makes you wonder," he said.
"Really makes you think."
Very true, Sheriff,
And it is an eschatological expectation
To learn what they actually
Know about us.

FRANKENSTEIN

Mary Shelley wrote FRANKENSTEIN as a metaphor
Telling us to carefully watch Science
Or it would create a veritable Monster.
Since, however, the public enjoys
Being frightened and shrieking,
New creatures have come forth
With dizzying regularity.
But by all accounts Science has had a wonderful career,
Giving us more than any prior civilization
For ease of living and comfort of life.
Yet, we might ask the enduring people
Of Nagasaki and Hiroshima
How it added to the splendor and brightness
Of their ordinary days.
No one could ever say that the Japanese
Did not know how to scream at the Monster.

> Mary Shelley (1797–1851), English novelist,
> wrote FRANKENSTEIN in 1818, and by 1945
> Science had produced atomic bombs,
> two of which were dropped on Japan.

NAAMAN IS CURED

This alien, muddy river,
And this trivial, superstitious ceremony!
My soldiers will hear of this.
They will say I am a poor, desperate man
Who will not accept his fate.
I'll be a laughingstock before I die.
When all the while I can take my sword
And slaughter everyone in sight!
Slice, hack, and cut
This useless water.
Not this death of rotting stumps!
I will tear out my heart first.
I am a fool to try this, but
Five . . . six . . . seven, and
My God-Mother's water opens,
And behold that-this-child's FLESH!

> The story of this soldier-leper in 2 Kings 5.

THE WINDOW

She died while I was opening the window
To look out on the lush, green yard.
The room was full of thoughts and feelings
And very much needed the Spring air.
I was not there,
But knew she died when the window
Would go up no further.
The light and the air told me so,
Even as I pushed until I could push no more.
It was years since I had seen her
And we had not talked or written,
But I knew she was dead
When I opened the window,
Panes splashed with spots of rain,
Yet clear enough for me
To see that she was dead,
As I held in my hands this
Mysterious, translucent thing
Reflecting what I saw and should have seen.

THE ROOM

A place where rooms get smaller,
A strange relationship.
She loved him for a moment.
Their time was oddly spent.

They touched but insincerely,
And then she stayed away.
'Twas best, they both repeated.
A minor price to pay.

And so the rooms grew smaller,
In fact, were closing in.
They stayed, but often wondered,
Where did it all begin.

IN THE DARK WOOD

Deep in the dark wood
They asked questions
Of the aging man.
He could only whisper
That at last they
Had come to him
As he knew they would.
There was nothing to be done now,
And he told them to leave
Him safely alone.
They complied and walked away,
Further and further, deeper and deeper
Into the dark and insubstantial wood
Where other old men
Were waiting to be found.

THE TABLEAU

The man sits on the edge of the gray bed
Caressing his dead wife.
The children peer through the cracked door
Not knowing why Mother
Does not call to them,
Or reach out her gentle hand.
The weighty burden has crushingly come,
No word, no warning, no interpretation,
For those little ones in the dim doorway
Watching the tearful love
Of a bedside manner
Which will leave them there
Until a caring therapist helps open
All the way,
Exposing them to its dark and blazing light.

FALLING INTO MONA LISA

Through oceans of sleep I could not dream,
But then I dreamed
That as I stared, she called me to come.
Stumbling forward, I aimed for the mouth,
The wisp of smile, the ancient lips
Begging to be kissed.
I am a post-modern man
And our sensibilities will never match.
Whatever would we talk about,
Or so I thought until
I fell against the canvas,
That greatest artistic mystery of all.
It was only a touch, a brush,
A thing lighter than air.
And then I withdrew.
Our eyes met.
I moved.
They met again.
I turned to go,
But wherever I go
She will be there.
Whatever I do or think I do,
She will see.
Child, woman, mother,
I will never be the same.
I weep,
For you will never hold me.

EVOLUTION: THE DAWN OF TIME

A million years ago the sky was gray.
The ceaseless rain was pelting spongy trees.
The mass of rock was cooling day by day.
Plants blossomed as they watched the pregnant seas.

In time the heavy atmosphere grew thin.
The vaporous clouds began to break and part.
The living rays of life were filtered in,
And ricocheted into the earth's deep heart.

Evolving from the cells of their first slime,
The many-shaped creatures plod their way.
In that long sea, oblivious to time,
Cold currents caused the thriving plants to sway.

One day, influenced by an unseen source,
A solitary creature turned his nose
To vertical from horizontal course.
Up from the deep and murky depths it rose.

Up, up, the tail and fins the being drove,
Up toward the lighter water and the sky.
Up, up, with every energy he strove.
And then the shock as eye met burning eye.

How cautiously he viewed the foreign sight:
Beyond the waves a blurry mass of green.
The strange attraction of the glowing light.
The two eyes seeing also being seen.

By day, the creature swam a constant path.
By night it scurried to the refuge cave.
Each morning toward the yellow flame he climbed.
And then the top fin broke the rolling wave.

The blazing sun began to burn its soul.
The heart of fire and of the creature wed.
The surface broke, into the air he leapt,
And toward the ball he thrust his scaly head.

ADAM AND THE DANGER OF SLEEP

Genesis 2:21: "Then the Lord God caused a deep sleep to come upon the man."

He struggled and fought
To maintain the control
That was always his.
But slowly he slipped into
What would become a recurring, nocturnal
Visit with death.
He dreamed.
And in his dream he saw
A phenomenal, ephemeral thing
Which he could touch and embrace.
Exhaustively satiated, he heard
The creature speak:
"There must be more than this! There must!"
He responded, tall, determined, erect,
And dully pointed to the exudate and slow-healing gash.
"Not that!" she chided, "Not that."
And looking to the East,
She stopped as she espied
An aura of something new and glossy and leafy.
Reluctantly, he joined her,
And clutching hands, they ambled incautiously
Toward the icy, cold theology
Of their catastrophic and eternal fate.

THOMAS RONALD VAUGHAN has spent his career in healthcare and ministry, serving parishes in the United Church of Christ and the Presbyterian Church USA. This is his sixth book of poetry, and he has written three works of Theology. Most of these writings are available on Wipf and Stock imprints. Vaughan lives with his wife, Jayne, in western North Carolina.

www.ingramcontent.com/pod-product-compliance
Lightning Source LLC
Chambersburg PA
CBHW071726040426
42446CB00011B/2243